This book belongs to-

_____

_____

_____

_____

2019 BLOG PLANNER

Published by Journal Spark
First Edition
Illustrations and designs Copyright 2019 Journal Spark
www.journalspark.com

Let's face it, you are busy! It's not your fault, with so much going on it is easy to get off track and lose focus with your blog.

Just follow the steps laid out for you in each section of this planner and stay on track all year long!

☺ THANK YOU so much for purchasing the Blog Yearly Planner. To show our appreciation, we have a great **FREE** resource for you: **Top 10 Blogging Mistakes to Avoid**

Simply visit:
journalspark.info/blog

Make sure you are not making any of these mistakes, especially #5 & #8!

Questions or feedback? Contact us at:
becky@journalspark.com

Blog Planner

BLOG TITLE:

DOMAIN:

TARGET AUDIENCE:

NICHE OVERVIEW:

MAIN FOCUS:

PRIMARY KEYWORDS:

MAIN TRAFFIC SOURCES:

Blog Controls

ADMIN LOGIN:

AFFILIATE ACCOUNTS:

ADVERTISER ACCOUNTS:

HOSTING ACCOUNT LOGIN:

IMPORTANT CONTACTS

PARTNERS:

OTHER:

Social Media

TWITTER

FACEBOOK

INSTAGRAM

PINTEREST

OTHER

OTHER

OTHER

OTHER

Brand Creation

SLOGAN / TAGLINE:

_____

NICHE SUMMARY:

_____

_____

_____

_____

HOW MY BLOG PROVIDES VALUE:

_____

_____

_____

MISSION STATEMENT:

_____

_____

_____

_____

WRITING & CONTENT STYLE:

_____

_____

_____

6 WORDS TO DESCRIBE MY BLOG:

_____   _____

_____   _____

_____   _____

Blog Design

BLOG STYLE OBJECTIVE:

THEME USED:

BASE COLOR SCHEME:

PRIMARY FONTS USED:

LOGO / GRAPHIC DESIGNER:

DESIGN CHECKLIST:

- Verify responsive design
- Create 404 landing page
- Install contact form & opt in
- Create advertiser side widgets
- Test links in navigation menu
- Install Cookie Permission Plugin
- Install Privacy Agreement

PLUGIN CHECKLIST:

- Install SEO plugin
- Install WP Total Cache
- Install social sharing plugin
- Install WP Forms
- Install Google Analytics
- Install Backup Plugin
- Install Opt-in Plugin

Affiliate Accounts

ADVERTISER ACCOUNTS:

AFFILIATE ACCOUNTS:

Marketing Planner

TOP TRAFFIC CHANNELS:

MARKETING TO DO LIST:

FREE ADVERTISING IDEAS:

PAID ADVERTISING IDEAS:

January

TASKS, MARKETING, ENGAGEMENT & MONETIZATION

CONTENT IDEAS

PROMOTION IDEAS

TOP PRIORITIES

MONTHLY FOCUS

MONETIZATION IDEAS

Monthly Goals

MAIN OBJECTIVE:

GOAL:

ACTION STEPS:

GOAL:

ACTION STEPS:

GOAL:

ACTION STEPS:

TRAFFIC STATS:

MAILING LIST SUBSCRIBERS:

Content Planner

POST TITLE:

PUBLICATION DATE:

TARGETED KEYWORDS:

TO DO CHECKLIST:

- Research Topic
- Pinpoint Target Audience
- Choose target keywords
- Optimize for search engines
- Link to other blog post
- Create post images
- Proofread & Edit Post
- Schedule Post Date

SOCIAL SHARING: (circle all that apply)

TOPIC OUTLINE:

NOTES:

Content Planner

CATEGORY:

RESOURCE LINKS:

GRAPHICS/IMAGES:

KEY POINTS:

SEO CHECKLIST:

- Primary keyword in post title
- Secondary keyword in sub-title
- Keyword in first paragraph
- Word count > 1000 words
- 1-2 Outbound Links
- Internal Link Structure
- Post URL includes keywords
- Meta description added
- Post includes images
- Post includes sub-headlines
- Social sharing enabled

NOTES:

Post Planner

WEEK OF: _____

TYPE: ARTICLE: ☐   TUTORIAL: ☐   REVIEW: ☐   GUEST POST: ☐

PUBLICATION DATE:

TITLE: _____

CATEGORY: _____

KEYWORDS: _____

NOTES: _____

PUBLICATION DATE:

TITLE: _____

CATEGORY: _____

KEYWORDS: _____

NOTES: _____

PUBLICATION DATE:

TITLE: _____

CATEGORY: _____

KEYWORDS: _____

NOTES: _____

Post Planner

WEEK OF: _____

TYPE: ARTICLE: ☐ TUTORIAL: ☐ REVIEW: ☐ GUEST POST: ☐

PUBLICATION DATE:

TITLE:

CATEGORY:

KEYWORDS:

NOTES:

LIST BUILDING PROGRESS:

 # SUBSCRIBERS: _____ **EMAILED THIS WEEK** ✉

SOCIAL MEDIA PROMO THIS WEEK:

☐ 🐦 ☐ f ☐ P ☐ 📷 ☐ ▶ in ☐ 8+

EXTERNAL LINKS:

INTERNAL LINKS:

PRODUCTS PROMOTED:

Affiliate Disclaimer Included

Guest Post Planner

POST TITLE:

PUBLISH DATE:	CATEGORY:

MAIN TOPIC:

POST SUMMARY:

KEY POINTS:

- ☐ _____
- ☐ _____
- ☐ _____
- ☐ _____

INCLUDED LINKS:

_____

_____

SHARED ON:

FACEBOOK ☐	INSTAGRAM ☐
TWITTER ☐	PINTEREST ☐
☐	☐

TAGS & KEYWORDS:

_____ ☐

_____ ☐

_____ ☐

# OF COMMENTS:	# OF TRACKBACKS:

NOTES:

Marketing Planner

TOP TRAFFIC CHANNELS:

MARKETING TO DO LIST:

FREE ADVERTISING IDEAS:

PAID ADVERTISING IDEAS:

Marketing Tracker

PROMOTIONAL IDEAS:

MARKETING TO DO:

SOCIAL MEDIA GROWTH TRACKER:

	BEFORE:	AFTER:
f		
Instagram		
Twitter		
Pinterest		
YouTube		
OTHER:		

LIST BUILDING & ENGAGEMENT:

MAILING LIST SUBSCRIBERS:	
# OF EMAILS SENT TO SUBSCRIBERS:	
# OF NEW BLOG POSTS THIS WEEK:	
# OF COMPLETED GUEST POSTS:	

NOTES:

February

TASKS, MARKETING, ENGAGEMENT & MONETIZATION

CONTENT IDEAS

PROMOTION IDEAS

TOP PRIORITIES

MONTHLY FOCUS

MONETIZATION RESOURCES

Monthly Goals

MAIN OBJECTIVE:

GOAL:

ACTION STEPS:

GOAL:

ACTION STEPS:

GOAL:

ACTION STEPS:

TRAFFIC STATS:

MAILING LIST SUBSCRIBERS:

Content Planner

POST TITLE:

PUBLICATION DATE:

TARGETED KEYWORDS:

TO DO CHECKLIST:

Research Topic

Pinpoint Target Audience

Choose target keywords

Optimize for search engines

Link to other blog post

Create post images

Proofread & Edit Post

Schedule Post Date

SOCIAL SHARING: (circle all that apply)

NOTES:

TOPIC OUTLINE:

Content Planner

CATEGORY:

RESOURCE LINKS:

GRAPHICS/IMAGES:

KEY POINTS:

SEO CHECKLIST:

- [ ] Primary keyword in post title
- [ ] Secondary keyword in sub-title
- [ ] Keyword in first paragraph
- [ ] Word count > 1000 words
- [ ] 1-2 Outbound Links
- [ ] Internal Link Structure
- [ ] Post URL includes keywords
- [ ] Meta description added
- [ ] Post includes images
- [ ] Post includes sub-headlines
- [ ] Social sharing enabled

NOTES:

Post Planner

WEEK OF: _____

TYPE: ARTICLE: ☐ TUTORIAL: ☐ REVIEW: ☐ GUEST POST: ☐

PUBLICATION DATE:

TITLE: _____

CATEGORY: _____

KEYWORDS: _____

NOTES: _____

PUBLICATION DATE:

TITLE: _____

CATEGORY: _____

KEYWORDS: _____

NOTES: _____

PUBLICATION DATE:

TITLE: _____

CATEGORY: _____

KEYWORDS: _____

NOTES: _____

Post Planner

WEEK OF: _____

TYPE: ARTICLE: ☐ TUTORIAL: ☐ REVIEW: ☐ GUEST POST: ☐

PUBLICATION DATE:

TITLE: _____

CATEGORY: _____

KEYWORDS: _____

NOTES: _____

_____

LIST BUILDING PROGRESS:

 # SUBSCRIBERS: _____ ☐ **EMAILED THIS WEEK** ✉

SOCIAL MEDIA PROMO THIS WEEK:

☐ 🐦 ☐ f ☐ 📌 ☐ 📷 ☐ ▶ ☐ in ☐ g+

EXTERNAL LINKS:

INTERNAL LINKS:

PRODUCTS PROMOTED:

☐ Affiliate Disclaimer Included

Guest Post Planner

POST TITLE:

PUBLISH DATE:	CATEGORY:

MAIN TOPIC:

POST SUMMARY:

KEY POINTS:

- ☐ _____
- ☐ _____
- ☐ _____
- ☐ _____

INCLUDED LINKS:

_____

_____

SHARED ON:

FACEBOOK ☐	INSTAGRAM ☐
TWITTER ☐	PINTEREST ☐
☐	☐

TAGS & KEYWORDS:

_____ ☐

_____ ☐

_____ ☐

 # OF COMMENTS: | **# OF TRACKBACKS:**

NOTES:

Marketing Planner

TOP TRAFFIC CHANNELS:

MARKETING TO DO LIST:

FREE ADVERTISING IDEAS:

PAID ADVERTISING IDEAS:

Marketing Tracker

PROMOTIONAL STRATEGIES TO MAXIMIZE EXPOSURE

PROMOTIONAL IDEAS:

MARKETING TO DO:

SOCIAL MEDIA GROWTH TRACKER:

	BEFORE:	AFTER:
f		
(instagram)		
(twitter)		
(pinterest)		
(youtube)		
OTHER:		

LIST BUILDING & ENGAGEMENT:

MAILING LIST
SUBSCRIBERS:

OF EMAILS SENT
TO SUBSCRIBERS:

OF NEW BLOG
POSTS THIS WEEK:

OF COMPLETED
GUEST POSTS:

NOTES:

March

TASKS, MARKETING, ENGAGEMENT & MONETIZATION

CONTENT IDEAS

PROMOTION IDEAS

TOP PRIORITIES

MONTHLY FOCUS

MONETIZATION RESOURCES

Monthly Goals

MAIN OBJECTIVE:

GOAL:

ACTION STEPS:

GOAL:

ACTION STEPS:

GOAL:

ACTION STEPS:

TRAFFIC STATS:

MAILING LIST SUBSCRIBERS:

Content Planner

POST TITLE:

PUBLICATION DATE:

TARGETED KEYWORDS:

TO DO CHECKLIST:

- Research Topic
- Pinpoint Target Audience
- Choose target keywords
- Optimize for search engines
- Link to other blog post
- Create post images
- Proofread & Edit Post
- Schedule Post Date

SOCIAL SHARING: (circle all that apply)

TOPIC OUTLINE:

NOTES:

Content Planner

CATEGORY:

RESOURCE LINKS:

GRAPHICS/IMAGES:

KEY POINTS:

SEO CHECKLIST:

- Primary keyword in post title
- Secondary keyword in sub-title
- Keyword in first paragraph
- Word count > 1000 words
- 1-2 Outbound Links
- Internal Link Structure
- Post URL includes keywords
- Meta description added
- Post includes images
- Post includes sub-headlines
- Social sharing enabled

NOTES:

Post Planner

WEEK OF: _____

TYPE: ARTICLE: ☐ TUTORIAL: ☐ REVIEW: ☐ GUEST POST: ☐

PUBLICATION DATE:

TITLE: _____

CATEGORY: _____

KEYWORDS: _____

NOTES: _____

PUBLICATION DATE:

TITLE: _____

CATEGORY: _____

KEYWORDS: _____

NOTES: _____

PUBLICATION DATE:

TITLE: _____

CATEGORY: _____

KEYWORDS: _____

NOTES: _____

Post Planner

WEEK OF: _____

TYPE: ARTICLE: ☐ TUTORIAL: ☐ REVIEW: ☐ GUEST POST: ☐

PUBLICATION DATE:

TITLE: _____

CATEGORY: _____

KEYWORDS: _____

NOTES: _____

_____

LIST BUILDING PROGRESS:

 # SUBSCRIBERS: _____ ☐ **EMAILED THIS WEEK** ✉

SOCIAL MEDIA PROMO THIS WEEK:

☐ 🐦 ☐ f ☐ 𝓟 ☐ 📷 ☐ ▶ in ☐ g+

EXTERNAL LINKS:

INTERNAL LINKS:

PRODUCTS PROMOTED:

Affiliate Disclaimer Included

Guest Post Planner

POST TITLE:

PUBLISH DATE:	CATEGORY:

MAIN TOPIC:

POST SUMMARY:

KEY POINTS:

- ☐ _____
- ☐ _____
- ☐ _____
- ☐ _____

INCLUDED LINKS:

_____

_____

SHARED ON:

FACEBOOK ☐	INSTAGRAM ☐
TWITTER ☐	PINTEREST ☐
☐	☐

TAGS & KEYWORDS:

_____ ☐

_____ ☐

_____ ☐

# OF COMMENTS:	# OF TRACKBACKS:

NOTES:

Marketing Planner

TOP TRAFFIC CHANNELS:

MARKETING TO DO LIST:

FREE ADVERTISING IDEAS:

PAID ADVERTISING IDEAS:

Marketing Tracker

PROMOTIONAL STRATEGIES TO MAXIMIZE EXPOSURE

PROMOTIONAL IDEAS:

MARKETING TO DO:

SOCIAL MEDIA GROWTH TRACKER:

	BEFORE:	AFTER:
f		
Instagram		
Twitter		
Pinterest		
YouTube		
OTHER:		

LIST BUILDING & ENGAGEMENT:

MAILING LIST SUBSCRIBERS:

 # OF EMAILS SENT TO SUBSCRIBERS:

 # OF NEW BLOG POSTS THIS WEEK:

 # OF COMPLETED GUEST POSTS:

NOTES:

April

TASKS, MARKETING, ENGAGEMENT & MONETIZATION

CONTENT IDEAS

PROMOTION IDEAS

TOP PRIORITIES

MONTHLY FOCUS

MONETIZATION RESOURCES

Monthly Goals

MAIN OBJECTIVE:

GOAL:

ACTION STEPS:

GOAL:

ACTION STEPS:

GOAL:

ACTION STEPS:

TRAFFIC STATS:

MAILING LIST SUBSCRIBERS:

Content Planner

POST TITLE:

PUBLICATION DATE:

TARGETED KEYWORDS:

TO DO CHECKLIST:

- Research Topic
- Pinpoint Target Audience
- Choose target keywords
- Optimize for search engines
- Link to other blog post
- Create post images
- Proofread & Edit Post
- Schedule Post Date

SOCIAL SHARING: (circle all that apply)

TOPIC OUTLINE:

NOTES:

Content Planner

CATEGORY:

_____

RESOURCE LINKS:

_____

_____

_____

GRAPHICS/IMAGES:

_____

KEY POINTS:

_____

_____

_____

_____

_____

_____

SEO CHECKLIST:

- [ ] Primary keyword in post title
- [ ] Secondary keyword in sub-title
- [ ] Keyword in first paragraph
- [ ] Word count > 1000 words
- [ ] 1-2 Outbound Links
- [ ] Internal Link Structure
- [ ] Post URL includes keywords
- [ ] Meta description added
- [ ] Post includes images
- [ ] Post includes sub-headlines
- [ ] Social sharing enabled

NOTES:

Post Planner

WEEK OF: _____

TYPE: ARTICLE: ☐   TUTORIAL: ☐   REVIEW: ☐   GUEST POST: ☐

PUBLICATION DATE:

TITLE: _____

CATEGORY: _____

KEYWORDS: _____

NOTES: _____

_____

PUBLICATION DATE:

TITLE: _____

CATEGORY: _____

KEYWORDS: _____

NOTES: _____

_____

PUBLICATION DATE:

TITLE: _____

CATEGORY: _____

KEYWORDS: _____

NOTES: _____

_____

Post Planner

WEEK OF: _____

TYPE: ARTICLE: ☐   TUTORIAL: ☐   REVIEW: ☐   GUEST POST: ☐

PUBLICATION DATE:

TITLE: _____

CATEGORY: _____

KEYWORDS: _____

NOTES: _____

_____

LIST BUILDING PROGRESS:

 # SUBSCRIBERS: _____ ☐ **EMAILED THIS WEEK** ✉

SOCIAL MEDIA PROMO THIS WEEK:

☐ 🐦   ☐ f   ☐ 𝓟   ☐ 📷   ☐ ▶   ☐ in   ☐ g+

EXTERNAL LINKS:

INTERNAL LINKS:

PRODUCTS PROMOTED:

☐ Affiliate Disclaimer Included

Guest Post Planner

POST TITLE:

PUBLISH DATE: CATEGORY:

MAIN TOPIC:

POST SUMMARY:

KEY POINTS:

INCLUDED LINKS:

SHARED ON:

FACEBOOK   INSTAGRAM

TWITTER   PINTEREST

TAGS & KEYWORDS:

OF COMMENTS: # OF TRACKBACKS:

NOTES:

Marketing Planner

TOP TRAFFIC CHANNELS:

MARKETING TO DO LIST:

FREE ADVERTISING IDEAS:

PAID ADVERTISING IDEAS:

Marketing Tracker

PROMOTIONAL IDEAS:

MARKETING TO DO:

SOCIAL MEDIA GROWTH TRACKER:

	BEFORE:	AFTER:
f		
Instagram		
Twitter		
Pinterest		
YouTube		
OTHER:		

LIST BUILDING & ENGAGEMENT:

MAILING LIST SUBSCRIBERS:	
# OF EMAILS SENT TO SUBSCRIBERS:	
# OF NEW BLOG POSTS THIS WEEK:	
# OF COMPLETED GUEST POSTS:	

NOTES:

May

TASKS, MARKETING, ENGAGEMENT & MONETIZATION

CONTENT IDEAS	PROMOTION IDEAS

TOP PRIORITIES

MONTHLY FOCUS	MONETIZATION RESOURCES

Monthly Goals

MAIN OBJECTIVE:

GOAL:

ACTION STEPS:

GOAL:

ACTION STEPS:

GOAL:

ACTION STEPS:

TRAFFIC STATS:

MAILING LIST SUBSCRIBERS:

Content Planner

POST TITLE:

PUBLICATION DATE:

TARGETED KEYWORDS:

TO DO CHECKLIST:

- Research Topic
- Pinpoint Target Audience
- Choose target keywords
- Optimize for search engines
- Link to other blog post
- Create post images
- Proofread & Edit Post
- Schedule Post Date

SOCIAL SHARING: (circle all that apply)

TOPIC OUTLINE:

NOTES:

Content Planner

CATEGORY:

RESOURCE LINKS:

GRAPHICS/IMAGES:

KEY POINTS:

SEO CHECKLIST:

- Primary keyword in post title
- Secondary keyword in sub-title
- Keyword in first paragraph
- Word count > 1000 words
- 1-2 Outbound Links
- Internal Link Structure
- Post URL includes keywords
- Meta description added
- Post includes images
- Post includes sub-headlines
- Social sharing enabled

NOTES:

Post Planner

WEEK OF: _____

TYPE: ARTICLE: ☐   TUTORIAL: ☐   REVIEW: ☐   GUEST POST: ☐

PUBLICATION DATE:

TITLE: _____

CATEGORY: _____

KEYWORDS: _____

NOTES: _____

_____

PUBLICATION DATE:

TITLE: _____

CATEGORY: _____

KEYWORDS: _____

NOTES: _____

_____

PUBLICATION DATE:

TITLE: _____

CATEGORY: _____

KEYWORDS: _____

NOTES: _____

_____

Post Planner

WEEK OF: _____

TYPE: ARTICLE: ☐   TUTORIAL: ☐   REVIEW: ☐   GUEST POST: ☐

PUBLICATION DATE:

TITLE: _____

CATEGORY: _____

KEYWORDS: _____

NOTES: _____

LIST BUILDING PROGRESS:

 # SUBSCRIBERS: _____   ☐   **EMAILED THIS WEEK** ✉

SOCIAL MEDIA PROMO THIS WEEK:

☐ 🐦   ☐ f   ☐ 𝓟   ☐ 📷   ☐ ▶   ☐ in   ☐ g+

EXTERNAL LINKS:

INTERNAL LINKS:

PRODUCTS PROMOTED:

Affiliate Disclaimer Included

Guest Post Planner

POST TITLE:

PUBLISH DATE:

CATEGORY:

MAIN TOPIC:

POST SUMMARY:

KEY POINTS:

- ☐ _____
- ☐ _____
- ☐ _____
- ☐ _____

INCLUDED LINKS:

_____

_____

SHARED ON:

FACEBOOK	☐	INSTAGRAM	☐
TWITTER	☐	PINTEREST	☐
	☐		☐

TAGS & KEYWORDS:

_____ ☐

_____ ☐

_____ ☐

 # OF COMMENTS:

 # OF TRACKBACKS:

NOTES:

Marketing Planner

TOP TRAFFIC CHANNELS:

MARKETING TO DO LIST:

FREE ADVERTISING IDEAS:

PAID ADVERTISING IDEAS:

Marketing Tracker

PROMOTIONAL IDEAS:

MARKETING TO DO:

SOCIAL MEDIA GROWTH TRACKER:

	BEFORE:	AFTER:
f		
Instagram		
Twitter		
Pinterest		
YouTube		
OTHER:		

LIST BUILDING & ENGAGEMENT:

MAILING LIST SUBSCRIBERS:

 # OF EMAILS SENT TO SUBSCRIBERS:

 # OF NEW BLOG POSTS THIS WEEK:

 # OF COMPLETED GUEST POSTS:

NOTES:

June

TASKS, MARKETING, ENGAGEMENT & MONETIZATION

CONTENT IDEAS

PROMOTION IDEAS

TOP PRIORITIES

MONTHLY FOCUS

MONETIZATION RESOURCES

Monthly Goals

MAIN OBJECTIVE:

GOAL:

ACTION STEPS:

GOAL:

ACTION STEPS:

GOAL:

ACTION STEPS:

TRAFFIC STATS:

MAILING LIST SUBSCRIBERS:

Content Planner

POST TITLE:

PUBLICATION DATE:

TARGETED KEYWORDS:

TO DO CHECKLIST:

Research Topic

Pinpoint Target Audience

Choose target keywords

Optimize for search engines

Link to other blog post

Create post images

Proofread & Edit Post

Schedule Post Date

SOCIAL SHARING: (circle all that apply)

NOTES:

TOPIC OUTLINE:

Content Planner

CATEGORY:

RESOURCE LINKS:

GRAPHICS/IMAGES:

KEY POINTS:

SEO CHECKLIST:

- [ ] Primary keyword in post title
- [ ] Secondary keyword in sub-title
- [ ] Keyword in first paragraph
- [ ] Word count > 1000 words
- [ ] 1-2 Outbound Links
- [ ] Internal Link Structure
- [ ] Post URL includes keywords
- [ ] Meta description added
- [ ] Post includes images
- [ ] Post includes sub-headlines
- [ ] Social sharing enabled

NOTES:

Post Planner

WEEK OF: _____

TYPE: ARTICLE: ☐ TUTORIAL: ☐ REVIEW: ☐ GUEST POST: ☐

PUBLICATION DATE:

TITLE: _____

CATEGORY: _____

KEYWORDS: _____

NOTES: _____

_____

PUBLICATION DATE:

TITLE: _____

CATEGORY: _____

KEYWORDS: _____

NOTES: _____

_____

PUBLICATION DATE:

TITLE: _____

CATEGORY: _____

KEYWORDS: _____

NOTES: _____

_____

Post Planner

WEEK OF: _____

TYPE: ARTICLE: ☐   TUTORIAL: ☐   REVIEW: ☐   GUEST POST: ☐

PUBLICATION DATE:

TITLE: _____

CATEGORY: _____

KEYWORDS: _____

NOTES: _____

_____

LIST BUILDING PROGRESS:

 # SUBSCRIBERS: _____   ☐   **EMAILED THIS WEEK** ✉

SOCIAL MEDIA PROMO THIS WEEK:

☐ 🐦   ☐ f   ☐ 𝓟   ☐ 📷   ☐ ▶   ☐ in   ☐ g+

EXTERNAL LINKS:

INTERNAL LINKS:

PRODUCTS PROMOTED:

☐ Affiliate Disclaimer Included

Guest Post Planner

POST TITLE:

PUBLISH DATE:	CATEGORY:

MAIN TOPIC:

POST SUMMARY:

KEY POINTS:

- [ ] _____
- [ ] _____
- [ ] _____
- [ ] _____

INCLUDED LINKS:	SHARED ON:		
_____		FACEBOOK [ ]	INSTAGRAM [ ]
_____		TWITTER [ ]	PINTEREST [ ]
		[ ]	[ ]

TAGS & KEYWORDS:	# OF COMMENTS:	# OF TRACKBACKS:
_____ [ ]		
_____ [ ]	**NOTES:**	
_____ [ ]		

Marketing Planner

TOP TRAFFIC CHANNELS:

MARKETING TO DO LIST:

FREE ADVERTISING IDEAS:

PAID ADVERTISING IDEAS:

Marketing Tracker

PROMOTIONAL IDEAS:

MARKETING TO DO:

SOCIAL MEDIA GROWTH TRACKER:

	BEFORE:	AFTER:
f		
Instagram		
Twitter		
Pinterest		
YouTube		
OTHER:		

LIST BUILDING & ENGAGEMENT:

MAILING LIST SUBSCRIBERS:

OF EMAILS SENT TO SUBSCRIBERS:

OF NEW BLOG POSTS THIS WEEK:

OF COMPLETED GUEST POSTS:

NOTES:

July

TASKS, MARKETING, ENGAGEMENT & MONETIZATION

CONTENT IDEAS

PROMOTION IDEAS

TOP PRIORITIES

MONTHLY FOCUS

MONETIZATION RESOURCES

Monthly Goals

MAIN OBJECTIVE:

GOAL:

ACTION STEPS:

GOAL:

ACTION STEPS:

GOAL:

ACTION STEPS:

TRAFFIC STATS:

MAILING LIST SUBSCRIBERS:

Content Planner

POST TITLE:

PUBLICATION DATE:

TARGETED KEYWORDS:

TO DO CHECKLIST:

Research Topic

Pinpoint Target Audience

Choose target keywords

Optimize for search engines

Link to other blog post

Create post images

Proofread & Edit Post

Schedule Post Date

SOCIAL SHARING: (circle all that apply)

NOTES:

TOPIC OUTLINE:

Content Planner

CATEGORY:

RESOURCE LINKS:

GRAPHICS/IMAGES:

KEY POINTS:

SEO CHECKLIST:

- [ ] Primary keyword in post title
- [ ] Secondary keyword in sub-title
- [ ] Keyword in first paragraph
- [ ] Word count > 1000 words
- [ ] 1-2 Outbound Links
- [ ] Internal Link Structure
- [ ] Post URL includes keywords
- [ ] Meta description added
- [ ] Post includes images
- [ ] Post includes sub-headlines
- [ ] Social sharing enabled

NOTES:

Post Planner

WEEK OF: _____

TYPE: ARTICLE: ☐   TUTORIAL: ☐   REVIEW: ☐   GUEST POST: ☐

PUBLICATION DATE:

TITLE: _____

CATEGORY: _____

KEYWORDS: _____

NOTES: _____

_____

PUBLICATION DATE:

TITLE: _____

CATEGORY: _____

KEYWORDS: _____

NOTES: _____

_____

PUBLICATION DATE:

TITLE: _____

CATEGORY: _____

KEYWORDS: _____

NOTES: _____

_____

Post Planner

WEEK OF: _____

TYPE: ARTICLE: ☐ TUTORIAL: ☐ REVIEW: ☐ GUEST POST: ☐

PUBLICATION DATE:

TITLE: _____

CATEGORY: _____

KEYWORDS: _____

NOTES: _____

_____

LIST BUILDING PROGRESS:

 # SUBSCRIBERS: _____ ☐ **EMAILED THIS WEEK** ✉️

SOCIAL MEDIA PROMO THIS WEEK:

☐ 🐦 ☐ f ☐ 📌 ☐ 📷 ☐ ▶️ in g+

EXTERNAL LINKS:

INTERNAL LINKS:

PRODUCTS PROMOTED:

☐ Affiliate Disclaimer Included

Guest Post Planner

POST TITLE:

PUBLISH DATE: CATEGORY:

MAIN TOPIC:

POST SUMMARY:

KEY POINTS:

- [ ] _____   - [ ] _____
- [ ] _____   - [ ] _____

INCLUDED LINKS:

_____

_____

SHARED ON:

FACEBOOK	☐	INSTAGRAM	☐
TWITTER	☐	PINTEREST	☐
	☐		☐

TAGS & KEYWORDS:

_____ ☐

_____ ☐

_____ ☐

 # OF COMMENTS: **# OF TRACKBACKS:**

NOTES:

Marketing Planner

TOP TRAFFIC CHANNELS:

MARKETING TO DO LIST:

FREE ADVERTISING IDEAS:

PAID ADVERTISING IDEAS:

Marketing Tracker

PROMOTIONAL STRATEGIES TO MAXIMIZE EXPOSURE

PROMOTIONAL IDEAS:

MARKETING TO DO:

SOCIAL MEDIA GROWTH TRACKER:

	BEFORE:	AFTER:
f		
Instagram		
Twitter		
Pinterest		
YouTube		
OTHER:		

LIST BUILDING & ENGAGEMENT:

MAILING LIST SUBSCRIBERS:

 # OF EMAILS SENT TO SUBSCRIBERS:

 # OF NEW BLOG POSTS THIS WEEK:

 # OF COMPLETED GUEST POSTS:

NOTES:

August

TASKS, MARKETING, ENGAGEMENT & MONETIZATION

CONTENT IDEAS

PROMOTION IDEAS

TOP PRIORITIES

MONTHLY FOCUS

MONETIZATION RESOURCES

Monthly Goals

MAIN OBJECTIVE:

GOAL:

ACTION STEPS:

GOAL:

ACTION STEPS:

GOAL:

ACTION STEPS:

TRAFFIC STATS:

MAILING LIST SUBSCRIBERS:

Content Planner

POST TITLE:

PUBLICATION DATE:

TARGETED KEYWORDS:

TO DO CHECKLIST:

Research Topic

Pinpoint Target Audience

Choose target keywords

Optimize for search engines

Link to other blog post

Create post images

Proofread & Edit Post

Schedule Post Date

SOCIAL SHARING: (circle all that apply)

NOTES:

TOPIC OUTLINE:

Content Planner

CATEGORY:

_____

RESOURCE LINKS:

_____

_____

_____

_____

GRAPHICS/IMAGES:

_____

_____

KEY POINTS:

_____

_____

_____

_____

_____

_____

SEO CHECKLIST:

- [ ] Primary keyword in post title
- [ ] Secondary keyword in sub-title
- [ ] Keyword in first paragraph
- [ ] Word count > 1000 words
- [ ] 1-2 Outbound Links
- [ ] Internal Link Structure
- [ ] Post URL includes keywords
- [ ] Meta description added
- [ ] Post includes images
- [ ] Post includes sub-headlines
- [ ] Social sharing enabled

NOTES:

Post Planner

WEEK OF: _____

TYPE: ARTICLE: ☐ TUTORIAL: ☐ REVIEW: ☑ GUEST POST: ☐

PUBLICATION DATE:

TITLE: _____

CATEGORY: _____

KEYWORDS: _____

NOTES: _____

_____

PUBLICATION DATE:

TITLE: _____

CATEGORY: _____

KEYWORDS: _____

NOTES: _____

_____

PUBLICATION DATE:

TITLE: _____

CATEGORY: _____

KEYWORDS: _____

NOTES: _____

_____

Post Planner

WEEK OF: _____

TYPE: ARTICLE: ☐   TUTORIAL: ☐   REVIEW: ☐   GUEST POST: ☐

PUBLICATION DATE:

TITLE: _____

CATEGORY: _____

KEYWORDS: _____

NOTES: _____

_____

LIST BUILDING PROGRESS:

 # SUBSCRIBERS: _____ ☐ **EMAILED THIS WEEK** ✉

SOCIAL MEDIA PROMO THIS WEEK:

☐ 🐦   ☐ f   ☐ 𝓟   ☐ 📷   ☐ ▶   ☐ in   ☐ 8+

EXTERNAL LINKS:

INTERNAL LINKS:

PRODUCTS PROMOTED:

☐ Affiliate Disclaimer Included

Guest Post Planner

POST TITLE:

PUBLISH DATE:	CATEGORY:

MAIN TOPIC:

POST SUMMARY:

KEY POINTS:

- ☐ _____ ☐ _____
- ☐ _____ ☐ _____

INCLUDED LINKS:	SHARED ON:	FACEBOOK ☐	INSTAGRAM ☐
		TWITTER ☐	PINTEREST ☐
		☐	☐

TAGS & KEYWORDS:	# OF COMMENTS:	# OF TRACKBACKS:
_____ ☐		
_____ ☐	**NOTES:**	
_____ ☐		

Marketing Planner

TOP TRAFFIC CHANNELS:

MARKETING TO DO LIST:

FREE ADVERTISING IDEAS:

PAID ADVERTISING IDEAS:

Marketing Tracker

PROMOTIONAL STRATEGIES TO MAXIMIZE EXPOSURE

PROMOTIONAL IDEAS:

MARKETING TO DO:

SOCIAL MEDIA GROWTH TRACKER:

	BEFORE:	AFTER:
f		
Instagram		
Twitter		
Pinterest		
YouTube		
OTHER:		

LIST BUILDING & ENGAGEMENT:

MAILING LIST SUBSCRIBERS:

OF EMAILS SENT TO SUBSCRIBERS:

OF NEW BLOG POSTS THIS WEEK:

OF COMPLETED GUEST POSTS:

NOTES:

September

TASKS, MARKETING, ENGAGEMENT & MONETIZATION

CONTENT IDEAS

PROMOTION IDEAS

TOP PRIORITIES

MONTHLY FOCUS

MONETIZATION RESOURCES

Monthly Goals

MAIN OBJECTIVE:

GOAL:

ACTION STEPS:

GOAL:

ACTION STEPS:

GOAL:

ACTION STEPS:

TRAFFIC STATS:

MAILING LIST SUBSCRIBERS:

Content Planner

POST TITLE:

PUBLICATION DATE:

TARGETED KEYWORDS:

TO DO CHECKLIST:

Research Topic

Pinpoint Target Audience

Choose target keywords

Optimize for search engines

Link to other blog post

Create post images

Proofread & Edit Post

Schedule Post Date

SOCIAL SHARING: (circle all that apply)

TOPIC OUTLINE:

NOTES:

Content Planner

CATEGORY:

RESOURCE LINKS:

GRAPHICS/IMAGES:

KEY POINTS:

SEO CHECKLIST:

- Primary keyword in post title
- Secondary keyword in sub-title
- Keyword in first paragraph
- Word count > 1000 words
- 1-2 Outbound Links
- Internal Link Structure
- Post URL includes keywords
- Meta description added
- Post includes images
- Post includes sub-headlines
- Social sharing enabled

NOTES:

Post Planner

WEEK OF: _____

TYPE: ARTICLE: ☐ TUTORIAL: ☐ REVIEW: ☐ GUEST POST: ☐

PUBLICATION DATE:

TITLE: _____

CATEGORY: _____

KEYWORDS: _____

NOTES: _____

_____

PUBLICATION DATE:

TITLE: _____

CATEGORY: _____

KEYWORDS: _____

NOTES: _____

_____

PUBLICATION DATE:

TITLE: _____

CATEGORY: _____

KEYWORDS: _____

NOTES: _____

_____

Post Planner

WEEK OF: _____

TYPE: ARTICLE: ☐ TUTORIAL: ☐ REVIEW: ☐ GUEST POST: ☐

PUBLICATION DATE:

TITLE: _____

CATEGORY: _____

KEYWORDS: _____

NOTES: _____

_____

LIST BUILDING PROGRESS:

 # SUBSCRIBERS: _____ ☐ **EMAILED THIS WEEK** ✉

SOCIAL MEDIA PROMO THIS WEEK:

☐ 🐦 ☐ f ☐ 𝓟 ☐ 📷 ☐ ▶ in ☐ g+

EXTERNAL LINKS:

PRODUCTS PROMOTED:

INTERNAL LINKS:

Affiliate Disclaimer Included

Guest Post Planner

POST TITLE:

PUBLISH DATE:	CATEGORY:

MAIN TOPIC:

POST SUMMARY:

KEY POINTS:

- ☐ _____
- ☐ _____
- ☐ _____
- ☐ _____

INCLUDED LINKS:

_____

_____

SHARED ON:

FACEBOOK ☐	INSTAGRAM ☐
TWITTER ☐	PINTEREST ☐
☐	☐

TAGS & KEYWORDS:

_____ ☐

_____ ☐

_____ ☐

# OF COMMENTS:	# OF TRACKBACKS:

NOTES:

Marketing Planner

TOP TRAFFIC CHANNELS:

MARKETING TO DO LIST:

FREE ADVERTISING IDEAS:

PAID ADVERTISING IDEAS:

Marketing Tracker

PROMOTIONAL STRATEGIES TO MAXIMIZE EXPOSURE

PROMOTIONAL IDEAS:

MARKETING TO DO:

SOCIAL MEDIA GROWTH TRACKER:

	BEFORE:	AFTER:
f		
Instagram		
Twitter		
Pinterest		
YouTube		
OTHER:		

LIST BUILDING & ENGAGEMENT:

MAILING LIST SUBSCRIBERS:

 # OF EMAILS SENT TO SUBSCRIBERS:

 # OF NEW BLOG POSTS THIS WEEK:

 # OF COMPLETED GUEST POSTS:

NOTES:

October

TASKS, MARKETING, ENGAGEMENT & MONETIZATION

CONTENT IDEAS

PROMOTION IDEAS

TOP PRIORITIES

MONTHLY FOCUS

MONETIZATION RESOURCES

Monthly Goals

MAIN OBJECTIVE:

GOAL:

ACTION STEPS:

GOAL:

ACTION STEPS:

GOAL:

ACTION STEPS:

TRAFFIC STATS:

MAILING LIST SUBSCRIBERS:

Content Planner

POST TITLE:

PUBLICATION DATE:

TARGETED KEYWORDS:

TO DO CHECKLIST:

Research Topic

Pinpoint Target Audience

Choose target keywords

Optimize for search engines

Link to other blog post

Create post images

Proofread & Edit Post

Schedule Post Date

SOCIAL SHARING: (circle all that apply)

TOPIC OUTLINE:

NOTES:

Content Planner

CATEGORY:

RESOURCE LINKS:

GRAPHICS/IMAGES:

KEY POINTS:

SEO CHECKLIST:

- [ ] Primary keyword in post title
- [ ] Secondary keyword in sub-title
- [ ] Keyword in first paragraph
- [ ] Word count > 1000 words
- [ ] 1-2 Outbound Links
- [ ] Internal Link Structure
- [ ] Post URL includes keywords
- [ ] Meta description added
- [ ] Post includes images
- [ ] Post includes sub-headlines
- [ ] Social sharing enabled

NOTES:

Post Planner

WEEK OF: _____

TYPE: ARTICLE: ☐ TUTORIAL: ☐ REVIEW: ☐ GUEST POST: ☐

PUBLICATION DATE:

TITLE: _____

CATEGORY: _____

KEYWORDS: _____

NOTES: _____

PUBLICATION DATE:

TITLE: _____

CATEGORY: _____

KEYWORDS: _____

NOTES: _____

PUBLICATION DATE:

TITLE: _____

CATEGORY: _____

KEYWORDS: _____

NOTES: _____

Post Planner

WEEK OF: _____

TYPE: ARTICLE: ☐   TUTORIAL: ☐   REVIEW: ☐   GUEST POST: ☐

PUBLICATION DATE:

TITLE: _____

CATEGORY: _____

KEYWORDS: _____

NOTES: _____

_____

LIST BUILDING PROGRESS:

 # SUBSCRIBERS: _____   ☐   **EMAILED THIS WEEK** ✉

SOCIAL MEDIA PROMO THIS WEEK:

☐ 🐦   ☐ f   ☐ 🅿   ☐ 📷   ☐ ▶   ☐ in   ☐ g+

EXTERNAL LINKS:

INTERNAL LINKS:

PRODUCTS PROMOTED:

☐ Affiliate Disclaimer Included

Guest Post Planner

POST TITLE:

PUBLISH DATE:	CATEGORY:
MAIN TOPIC:	
POST SUMMARY:	

KEY POINTS:

- ☐ _____
- ☐ _____
- ☐ _____
- ☐ _____

INCLUDED LINKS:

_____

_____

SHARED ON:

FACEBOOK ☐	INSTAGRAM ☐
TWITTER ☐	PINTEREST ☐
☐	☐

TAGS & KEYWORDS:

_____ ☐

_____ ☐

_____ ☐

# OF COMMENTS:	# OF TRACKBACKS:

NOTES:

Marketing Planner

TOP TRAFFIC CHANNELS:

MARKETING TO DO LIST:

FREE ADVERTISING IDEAS:

PAID ADVERTISING IDEAS:

Marketing Tracker

PROMOTIONAL IDEAS:

MARKETING TO DO:

SOCIAL MEDIA GROWTH TRACKER:

	BEFORE:	AFTER:
f		
Instagram		
Twitter		
Pinterest		
YouTube		
OTHER:		

LIST BUILDING & ENGAGEMENT:

MAILING LIST SUBSCRIBERS:

OF EMAILS SENT TO SUBSCRIBERS:

OF NEW BLOG POSTS THIS WEEK:

OF COMPLETED GUEST POSTS:

NOTES:

November

TASKS, MARKETING, ENGAGEMENT & MONETIZATION

CONTENT IDEAS

PROMOTION IDEAS

TOP PRIORITIES

MONTHLY FOCUS

MONETIZATION RESOURCES

Monthly Goals

MAIN OBJECTIVE:

GOAL:

ACTION STEPS:

GOAL:

ACTION STEPS:

GOAL:

ACTION STEPS:

TRAFFIC STATS:

MAILING LIST SUBSCRIBERS:

Content Planner

POST TITLE:

PUBLICATION DATE:

TARGETED KEYWORDS:

TO DO CHECKLIST:

- Research Topic
- Pinpoint Target Audience
- Choose target keywords
- Optimize for search engines
- Link to other blog post
- Create post images
- Proofread & Edit Post
- Schedule Post Date

SOCIAL SHARING: (circle all that apply)

TOPIC OUTLINE:

NOTES:

Content Planner

CATEGORY:

RESOURCE LINKS:

GRAPHICS/IMAGES:

KEY POINTS:

SEO CHECKLIST:

- Primary keyword in post title
- Secondary keyword in sub-title
- Keyword in first paragraph
- Word count > 1000 words
- 1-2 Outbound Links
- Internal Link Structure
- Post URL includes keywords
- Meta description added
- Post includes images
- Post includes sub-headlines
- Social sharing enabled

NOTES:

Post Planner

WEEK OF: _____

TYPE: ARTICLE: ☐   TUTORIAL: ☐   REVIEW: ☐   GUEST POST: ☐

PUBLICATION DATE:

TITLE: _____

CATEGORY: _____

KEYWORDS: _____

NOTES: _____

_____

PUBLICATION DATE:

TITLE: _____

CATEGORY: _____

KEYWORDS: _____

NOTES: _____

_____

PUBLICATION DATE:

TITLE: _____

CATEGORY: _____

KEYWORDS: _____

NOTES: _____

_____

Post Planner

WEEK OF: _____

TYPE: ARTICLE: ☐   TUTORIAL: ☐   REVIEW: ☐   GUEST POST: ☐

PUBLICATION DATE:

TITLE: _____

CATEGORY: _____

KEYWORDS: _____

NOTES: _____

LIST BUILDING PROGRESS:

 # SUBSCRIBERS: _____   **EMAILED THIS WEEK** ✉

SOCIAL MEDIA PROMO THIS WEEK:

☐ 🐦   ☐ f   ☐ 𝕡   ☐ 📷   ☐ ▶   in   g+

EXTERNAL LINKS:

PRODUCTS PROMOTED:

INTERNAL LINKS:

Affiliate Disclaimer Included

Guest Post Planner

POST TITLE:

PUBLISH DATE:	CATEGORY:
MAIN TOPIC:	
POST SUMMARY:	

KEY POINTS:

- [ ] _____
- [ ] _____
- [ ] _____
- [ ] _____

INCLUDED LINKS:

_____

_____

SHARED ON:

FACEBOOK	[ ]	INSTAGRAM	[ ]
TWITTER	[ ]	PINTEREST	[ ]
	[ ]		[ ]

TAGS & KEYWORDS:

_____ [ ]

_____ [ ]

_____ [ ]

# OF COMMENTS:	# OF TRACKBACKS:

NOTES:

Marketing Planner

TOP TRAFFIC CHANNELS:

MARKETING TO DO LIST:

FREE ADVERTISING IDEAS:

PAID ADVERTISING IDEAS:

Marketing Tracker

PROMOTIONAL STRATEGIES TO MAXIMIZE EXPOSURE

PROMOTIONAL IDEAS:

MARKETING TO DO:

SOCIAL MEDIA GROWTH TRACKER:

	BEFORE:	AFTER:
f		
Instagram		
Twitter		
Pinterest		
YouTube		

OTHER:

LIST BUILDING & ENGAGEMENT:

MAILING LIST SUBSCRIBERS:	
# OF EMAILS SENT TO SUBSCRIBERS:	
# OF NEW BLOG POSTS THIS WEEK:	
# OF COMPLETED GUEST POSTS:	

NOTES:

December

TASKS, MARKETING, ENGAGEMENT & MONETIZATION

CONTENT IDEAS

PROMOTION IDEAS

TOP PRIORITIES

MONTHLY FOCUS

MONETIZATION RESOURCES

Monthly Goals

MAIN OBJECTIVE:

GOAL:

ACTION STEPS:

GOAL:

ACTION STEPS:

GOAL:

ACTION STEPS:

TRAFFIC STATS:

MAILING LIST SUBSCRIBERS:

Content Planner

POST TITLE:

PUBLICATION DATE:

TARGETED KEYWORDS:

TO DO CHECKLIST:

Research Topic

Pinpoint Target Audience

Choose target keywords

Optimize for search engines

Link to other blog post

Create post images

Proofread & Edit Post

Schedule Post Date

SOCIAL SHARING: (circle all that apply)

NOTES:

TOPIC OUTLINE:

Content Planner

CATEGORY:

RESOURCE LINKS:

GRAPHICS/IMAGES:

KEY POINTS:

SEO CHECKLIST:

- [ ] Primary keyword in post title
- [ ] Secondary keyword in sub-title
- [ ] Keyword in first paragraph
- [ ] Word count > 1000 words
- [ ] 1-2 Outbound Links
- [ ] Internal Link Structure
- [ ] Post URL includes keywords
- [ ] Meta description added
- [ ] Post includes images
- [ ] Post includes sub-headlines
- [ ] Social sharing enabled

NOTES:

Post Planner

WEEK OF: _____

TYPE: ARTICLE: ☐   TUTORIAL: ☐   REVIEW: ☐   GUEST POST: ☐

PUBLICATION DATE:

TITLE:

CATEGORY:

KEYWORDS:

NOTES:

PUBLICATION DATE:

TITLE:

CATEGORY:

KEYWORDS:

NOTES:

PUBLICATION DATE:

TITLE:

CATEGORY:

KEYWORDS:

NOTES:

Post Planner

WEEK OF: _____

TYPE: ARTICLE: ☐ TUTORIAL: ☐ REVIEW: ☐ GUEST POST: ☐

PUBLICATION DATE:

TITLE: _____

CATEGORY: _____

KEYWORDS: _____

NOTES: _____

_____

LIST BUILDING PROGRESS:

 # SUBSCRIBERS: _____ ☐ **EMAILED THIS WEEK** ✉

SOCIAL MEDIA PROMO THIS WEEK:

☐ 🐦 ☐ f ☐ 𝓟 ☐ 📷 ☐ ▶ ☐ in ☐ 8+

EXTERNAL LINKS:

INTERNAL LINKS:

PRODUCTS PROMOTED:

☐ Affiliate Disclaimer Included

Guest Post Planner

POST TITLE:

PUBLISH DATE:	CATEGORY:
MAIN TOPIC:	
POST SUMMARY:	

KEY POINTS:

- ☐
- ☐
- ☐
- ☐

INCLUDED LINKS:

SHARED ON:

FACEBOOK ☐	INSTAGRAM ☐
TWITTER ☐	PINTEREST ☐
☐	☐

TAGS & KEYWORDS:

- ☐
- ☐
- ☐

# OF COMMENTS:	# OF TRACKBACKS:

NOTES:

Marketing Planner

TOP TRAFFIC CHANNELS:

MARKETING TO DO LIST:

FREE ADVERTISING IDEAS:

PAID ADVERTISING IDEAS:

Marketing Tracker

PROMOTIONAL IDEAS:

MARKETING TO DO:

SOCIAL MEDIA GROWTH TRACKER:

BEFORE: AFTER:

OTHER:

LIST BUILDING & ENGAGEMENT:

MAILING LIST
SUBSCRIBERS:

OF EMAILS SENT
TO SUBSCRIBERS:

OF NEW BLOG
POSTS THIS WEEK:

OF COMPLETED
GUEST POSTS:

NOTES:

Made in the
USA
Middletown, DE